Torchwood

Also by Jill Magi:

Threads (Futurepoem)
Cadastral Map (Portable Press at Yo-Yo Labs)

Torchwood

Jill Magi

Shearsman Books
Exeter

Published in the United Kingdom in 2008 by
Shearsman Books Ltd
58 Velwell Road
Exeter EX4 4LD

www.shearsman.com

ISBN-13 978-1-905700-54-7

Acknowledgements
Poems in this collection have appeared, in various forms, in the following
journals and collections: *can we have our ball back?*, *Harp & Altar*, *Pierogi Press*,
Moria Poetry, *My Spaceship* from Cy Gist Press, and *Raised in a Barn*. Thanks
to the editors for their support. The poems "Day with divine ferocity,"
"From the wall, transparent," and "Turn, song" include language from
poems by Ange Mlinko. "9/24," in the long poem entitled "2002," takes
language from Andrea L. Smith's "Heteroglossia, 'common sense,' and social
memory," published in *American Ethnologist*, Volume 1, Number 2, May 2004.
"Torchwood, a lexicon" was self-published as a chapbook, and "Thinking a
Kite" is from a small handmade book, made in an edition of four.

cover art: Jill Magi
cover design: Darcy Doyle

This book is for Trina.

Contents

I.   Day with divine ferocity   9
     From the wall, transparent,   10
     Turn, song   11
     Against Space   12
     I am Climbing Innsbruck   14

II. Nival (ni´ vel): of or growing in or under snow.   17

III. Religious Sonnets   31

     Soy Products:
        They might be high in sodium but they are not meat.   33
     A Stone   34
     I had a baptism but not in a river.   35
     The Butcher   36
     "We had a Holy Ghost time together."   37
     Social Bound   38
     The Book and Bible House   39
     Life Sketches   40
     The Great Disappointment   41

IV. 2002   43

V.   Relationships   61

VI. Torchwood, a lexicon   69

VII. Thinking a Kite   77

I.

Day with divine ferocity

Carrying yellow between us
is pasture, soul—

beauty from the sun
is your exercise in dreaming, thinking.

Such days hatch tomorrow in my girlhood—

purple on gold, I may tell you
about church.

FROM THE WALL, TRANSPARENT,

I take a day.

Tell me to slide in
and drink your tea
lest I pour myself out.
       (I pour out my age with all wisdom
available.)

I wear a veil. They insist
at my lion's rage.

Turn, song

Answering a bee, the heart-sound, a motorcycle
or a sudden
silk.

Justice
powers my lover, a mouth
sickled by a kiss—

If words are a helmet

stop
crashing.

Against Space

Eating crickets at the conference about the future, they showed us *Soylent Green*. Chaos or escape, the crackers are people, and on the bus there I said I didn't get space travel. Across blue skies many shocking falls or what the planet needs. Florida being closer. For the expansion of knowledge, she was corrective and stern. Generation of lightsabers, asteroids, o-rings. Joey Rasinski's intricate rockets made sounds as he bent over, penciling. It stood for Gifted and Talented and I didn't want to go, my emphasis on charts, colors. Or he drew sharks. They gave us a problem to solve in groups about population and food, which was my least favorite until the transparencies. My ink spot was a pupil and though I was nervous, eyelashes dominating the space, still I was placed while Jennifer Johnston was not. Aim has never been. Jet and fast little space pod, I sleep. Earth below, looking soft and teary, problems, hazy blue and green seems delicate. She was my best friend. The curve, feminized, indicates welcoming or vulnerability and I have said gravity versus freedom. Unending distance, boulders hurl themselves toward me in the space before sleep, I spin. I admit limits especially pulled toward warmth rather than out, soil rather than. Heaven might be the black hole in Orion's belt if you can find it, no eating and no sex. I declined. Making sure statements. "NASA invents Velcro" was the first line of the first poem I wrote in a sociology class when wearing Birkenstocks he explained space research is tied to war. Always having felt under the sky, not particularly curious. Strong diagonal. Or much goes on inside the house, diffused. Why up is considered imagination and down is inscribed. A planetary landscape is barren, site of history, the prophet comes to revive and whether green or deformed, those creatures locate our civility. She from his rib and all that. Directed attention. Such as a fighting system, a hero, and honor is an agreed-upon concept, except that everyone loved her gun and most memorable were her braids, Victorian. Evil, usually shiny and anonymous with more horsepower and masks, moves in groups with larger guns, so that the upright opposition is necessarily analog, individual skill, personality, and god. We saw them falling and touched each other's skin everywhere possible at once explosive and many-pointed. Cold war t-shirts and swag. Stars or danger but both are about love and trying, an ideal. Either way, entering a channel requires mentoring. Marks. Exile. Ambrosia. To receive. A microscope of evidence waits. Not that I am against space or odyssey, rather the mists and groups. Within or among being favored over conquer and shape shift, not necessarily.

I am Climbing Innsbruck

I am climbing Innsbruck, I am pathways for skis and rabbit
stew, at the Uni halls of blue smoke bludgeoning, I am a castle
of Lederhosen, do you cook? or volleyball? I am stamped of my
passport, I am hot wine in iron, winter kettles of Strudel and by
myself I am a projection across silence.

I wildflower,
I Schnitzel,
I lace,
I crucifix and Vienna,
I Salzburg and tunnel,
I castle,
I gypsy,
I Christmas, very Christmas.

You do cooking,
you do German,
you do knitting and not the gypsies again,
you do all night on the lake and dawn on the knoll,
you do dumplings and dumplings and dumplings.

I am Edelweiss speaking American, I am stamps and Post,
I am skiing down a strong coffee, I am silence
and I am by the River Inn,
a wish for a pizza pie, I am needing Alpenrose tea or Excedrin

from America, I am rare in feeling and climbing the thin air,
dancing behind the locked door, American.

This is a night of snowing and snowing, these are wildflowers
yellowing a bike path by the River Inn, this is Café Central and
me sitting a strong long coffee, writing a café notebook hour after
hour, this is my postcard, this is the yodel of Lederhosen, this is the
valley and my silence, a silence and valley, my life so far behind but
it's snowing and locked doors are opening now, you could say that
this is not the wildflower end to the story, English of my dreams,
my dreams and dreaming in German, my speaking, this is my wild
fluency and a little literacy, this is me carrying a handmade basket
and a dictionary, this is the Wienerwald, a restaurant chain having
nothing to do with American hotdogs, O my basket dumpling, sing
low, sing high, sing wide for me.

Do you lace?
or a green sweater knit thickly?
or bake a good Brot?
a starter dough?
go to Ball? the dance
with gown and feathers?
do you girl or lady or even just sometimes
just a bit of sometimes woman
even if just sometimes American?
do you teaching?
do you? yes,
all night on the lake
the moon sings low, sings high, sings wide.

I am not by the lake of the moon, I am climbing Innsbruck,
I am lace and a walking stick for the hike up to Frau Hitt,
I am slinging a basket, I am hiking and climbing the locked door
my Schnitzel, I am two languages projecting, reflecting the
        moon and again.

II.

NIVAL (NI′ VEL):
of or growing in or under snow.

( )

A walk into what has eclipsed us.

Cutwork
absorbing

     "I feel barren"

                setting up for pause

( )

Fallen into   above.

pry
pockets of blue—

rain   toward

          "I did not expect—   "

( )

Neap tide fossil.

Folded stone
teases the boundary of blindness.

( )

From the cell—   electrical.

Retracted, she lost her humor.

( )

Spokes light the wheel. Hub,
a fascicle. Impulse to collect—

December dream
of a Cooper's hawk.
Yesterday, five buffleheads,
the merganser pair,
swoop of a cormorant
draws the horizon—
us,

( )

Warming—

enough god—

if

( )

Concave side of quiet

takes rooms out of confines

                              January enwreathes.

( )

potter wasp

equipoise

hollow-balance

"I am nothing absolutely."

floating rib

story

( )

Great black back gull coasting
northeast

I hold clouds
in windows   delight
in what is false.

Wisp to vein to
table-sky.

( )

Anchor-pulled,

whorled,

imbricate prayers

imagine edges.

( )

Wall-expansion after

grief

porous.

(Marginalia sustained the binding.)

( )

What is the substance of shadow?
(Atrium of disaster-sense.)
What is between the twenty-second and third hour?
(Crux. Roomage on all sides as burns glister—
temperature spike in the space
between winter and kiln.)

( )

Ideas about curled iron.
(About is around.) Month
vines its way

     capillary bed.

( )

Canyoned

tidemark

        ("I am—")

mirror

a moiré effect.

( )

Tree of bowls

turned

to hold—

( )

Arrow-cloud.

Drill bit traces
read "remove / place."

Marital sculpture.

( )

       required to say
that we came to an amicable agreement. Truth
on the hinge

              (sutured rock, signatures)

( )

Ivied house. Endless chatter.

Lived house. Still

questions pond
in the collar bone of the hill,
wintered.

( )

open   inching from

right to left

glass / sky

                              —unaware, leaning on left to right

( )

A bottle gourd is not round.
A battleground may be partially.

My apsis   your form.

(Take away this   )

( )

collective blur

ancient texts
having no space between words

sliding epiphanies
into the point
between

( )

Dripstone

                                                    / mass.

( )

Count ambition's stripes—

How much is will?
How much time?

Answer   automatic sculpture

III.

Religious Sonnets

SOY PRODUCTS:
THEY MIGHT BE HIGH IN SODIUM BUT THEY ARE NOT MEAT.

They are made by Loma Linda and Worthington Foods,
two Adventist companies like Harris Pine Mills,
where most of the Adventist academy poor kids
and kids of color worked to pay off their tuition,

or the Little Debbie factory near Southern College where
Jerry Makarovskyi from the Ukraine got his hand caught
in a roller and had to have reconstructive surgery
but they said he was never the same, the arm just hung there.

Some soy products are rubbery like what are called Skallops
and some of it, like NuMeat, is a mushy loaf, a kind of pâté
that you push out of the can by opening both ends and some
soy products are frozen like ChikSticks, which come six to a box,

shaped like tiny flat drumsticks or Stakelets, which my grandmother,
whose father was a butcher, used to make in a rich cream sauce.

A STONE

You are in the company of your twin sister
and another schoolmate
crossing a common in the city of Portland, Maine
in the 19th century.

A girl of thirteen years becomes angry at some trifle
and this girl throws a stone.
A stone is thrown and this stone hits you,
Ellen Harmon, on the nose.

You fall senseless to the ground,
stunned by the blow
and never to be the same after,
the visions come.

The origin of the religion you invented and I was born into.
"Because a stone was thrown."

I HAD A BAPTISM BUT NOT IN A RIVER.

It is required that the water covers me but not subtle like fog and I
dread it though I know that it will happen eventually, this
submersion, to be saved. Hymns play softly with high vibrato, the
sanctuary dimmer switch is on, and in the orange light my white robe

billows as I take steps down into the tank. I try to push the air out of
the top part of my gown with my hands. It is not cold. There are
pebble-sized weights sown into the hem so that the gown will not fly
up to the surface of the water. Underneath I wear my underwear and

a slip and once inside the tank I am afraid of the mechanics of it but
the pastor holds on to me. "Do you take the Lord as your personal
savior? Then I baptize you in the name of the Father, the Son, and
the Holy Ghost." *Whoosh.* My legs kick out from under me. Later,

I stand in front of the church, hair wet, feeling close to God, holding
my Certificate of Baptism and a new red leather Bible.

The Butcher

My great-grandfather, Otto Hartnagel, the butcher
who hated the Kaiser, forbade Bible studies in his house
and this was a problem for Emma Guhl Hartnagel,
my great-grandmother, a new convert with long red hair,

and soon after he forbade this he fell down
the cellar steps and broke his leg,
a serious accident at that time, requiring lots of bed rest.
Emma said that this was a sign from the Devil

and so he allowed their meetings after all,
though he never attended and would not convert.
On his deathbed, according to my grandmother,
he was full of cancer from all the meat and smoking and beer,

and when she asked him to give his heart to the Lord
he refused and told her to never bring up that baloney again.

"WE HAD A HOLY GHOST TIME TOGETHER."

It is true that they were accused of holy kissing, falling to the ground,
and shouting in Maine in the 19th century at the beginning of the
religion. This is according to the *Piscataquis Farmer*, which is devoted
to politics, agriculture, literature, morals, temperance, and news.

A witness said that the meeting appeared very irreligious,
having seen a man sit on the floor with a woman between his legs
and his arms around her. There were accusations of footwashing
between the sexes, creeping, hollering, holy kissing,

even women kissing women, holy laughing, and rebaptism,
but it was the no-work policy that was found most repulsive and
punishable. It is also likely that young Ellen Harmon fled the scene of
the arrest but most Adventists will deny this or they don't know, but

of course there is a Web site where the disgruntled apostate may
gather, though the endnotes look suspicious, academically speaking.

Social Bound

In the Adventist high school you are not allowed to hold hands
and the punishment for touching is called "social bound"
or "social" for short. As in: "Jill and E. were placed on social
this Tuesday after being discovered in the library stairwell.

They are social bound for two weeks." This is how the disciplinary
committee minutes would read and this would mean that you are not
allowed to talk with or look at or sit with each other. All of the
teachers read the minutes faithfully in order to enforce the

punishment and they know it was more than holding hands because
two weeks on social is severe. Except this never happened to me,
probably due to my whiteness and good grades. Everyone says that
the Bible teacher who wears polyester pants is having an affair with

his student-secretary from Ecuador who grades papers
in his tiny second floor office by the library.

The Book and Bible House

I buy all the young adult books set in Africa or Latin America where the missionaries try to shut down the witch doctor. I look for jungle scenes on the covers and inside, young girls are possessed with demons, tables float, and candles are blown out by spirits and the

Devil. The ghost of the grandmother terrorizes them until the girl learns how to pray and so her family is impressed with her new powers, how she falls to her knees and the chaos ceases, so they convert, wear shoes to the new cinderblock church where they sit on

benches and sing "Jesus Loves Me" but slowly, like a dirge, "in their traditional singing style." (The monthly Mission Spotlight slide show usually begins with the flight of a small plane over the jungle.) At the Book and Bible House I taste the veggie meat fried in giant plug-in

pans and at home I read that the missionaries have pet monkeys and servants. It is always unbearably hot, making the fruits large and juicy.

Life Sketches

This could be a preface for an autobiography
or the bridge of two influences.
But cohesion is not the desired,
this being an un-pulpit.

Writing grafts onto a life,
working itself out in the space provided,
allowing for the litany as it is long and wide.
There has always been an emphasis on the sentence:

thinking and memory, constructing a grammar,
yet doors open and close. Then, flipping gold-
edged pages, the perfume wafts up as I search my Bible.
Now, how you love their prayer books, their fringes

and lips whisper the sacred text, they sway across from you.
On the subway, they are Sabbath-keepers as you now are not.

The Great Disappointment

Yet to be connected to something spiritual is the issue, having left the tradition. "Pillow of no tradition." I have written this. The history of the search is long, back to when they purchased ascension robes and bands of like-believers gathered in fields to await His second coming;

it was called The Great Disappointment. They became a national joke. And after October of 1844, the missionaries become zealous, spreading out to Europe and elsewhere, complimenting the nationalist fervor in my grandfather's country where, as a young man,

he met an American Adventist, found the Lord, and as a former actor, made an excellent minister. Even I was a "student missionary" when, for a year, I went abroad and contemplated culture and self, resulting in the unraveling, leading to apostasy.

They would not ordain women so I wrote a resignation letter, my prayer-life still intact. I wrote every day in my missionary journal.

IV.

2002

9/20

In scarlet again I
give thistles
the length of
dreamy sparks

in slippers
blinded, I

      soft landing
on a well-placed beauty-bush
while scarlet again I
give mountains

9/21

About the gift of tongues,
disbelief clusters
around professionals
in suits
while some congregations
play light hammers
on nonsense glossaries
glued to the stage as
one or two semivowels
come into a glimpse of
glory-of-the-snow

9/23

snap
a line

soon
a bridge
will fabricate

sails sewn
there

the house
is paid

popular memory is especially composite, partial, and internally
contradictory

heteroglossia: the juxtaposition of competing voices

encounters between dominant, official, hegemonic, or national
memories and subaltern, private, popular, or subordinate history

an effective counter-hegemonic assault, he felt,
would require the articulation of a counter-hegemonic narrative

in his view, a prerequisite for such a narrative is coherence

but that composite quality may in fact be fertile ground for
dynamic change

9/26

he returned from the church
with a bag full of rustproof
nails and settled in comfortably

she took short naps
to alleviate the urge to chase
ambulances until it was her own
face that she recognized

he looked up at the crow's voice and
remarked that for such a blue sky
the curtains really should be white

9/27

his braids against the glass

she looked at my toes with misgiving
and across her middle read "workout"
while they held on to fingers
and he used two to skim each line
of an illegible newspaper

nothing went express
between Pacific/Atlantic

9/28

dusk wants
safety and a raise

our change
clasps at the latch,

staples the candidate and
alarm

9/29

rain in curved air
air of an elbow curve
did you see inside your day?

a shawl over her slouch
a slouch in a tunnel of air
bent into a productive chorus that
comes on strong   I still believe
in a fog-slow harbor

a transplanted fern
thrives outside the forest

10/1

the world is much with
accuracy and truth

being as precise as possible against
media-speak

the poet
preserving the range

or "the shame
of your own sound

results in the death of a language"
said Cecilia Vicuña

10/4

most shutters painted against white
a green door screened slamming
on a porch swinging out the hours
believing I am made of the desire
for open space

oh willow willow falling blurring
grace a childhood rope-
ladder up to the appletree of my first book

go north go north

10/5

the pressure distributes
the upper stretches
the horizon opens

wet is banished
routine suffers the same fate

water resistant
wind resistant
water resistant
wind resistant

the pressure distributes

10/7

these bubbles aren't bad said
she to the clock whose
alarm no longer

waking I have that button but won't

"hmmm"
low-grade pair of
"really?"

it is well
to lose sight of the shore to arrive

10/11

a flock
circles until they split
into two
rollercoasters and
back together at the bricked

I'm not discontent this October
despite the safety I was warned
about in September

10/12

long seeing
bridge-through, I don't

migrating on the train
courageous   our

fundamental goodness
free-floating

I theory inside
the experienced

10/14

and an English
teacher in
Spain and
a university
professor
and a painter
and a museum
curator on
sabbatical a park
ranger a monk

V.

Relationships

Family, lover, colleague. Notions, veneers, nation. Teeth of no health insurance.

A boom can be a microphone affixed to a pole and not an explosion.

Shadows, we sweep at them constantly and on the table is chocolate, newspapers, commentary, and vastly different pay stubs.

I lean in to you and wish to love you perfectly.

Suffer, tumble, strive, the right shoes, and vacation.

At the table, conference and always pretty, the fixed.

Shimmer of repulsion or fairy tale of cleavage.

I count pleasures like cream, sipping, speaking. I like fashion as well.

All the hymns you and I know as his headboard knocks against our wall, the slap when he coughs, our neighbor.

The most racist of all positions at the staff meeting is to tell us about your shocking talent if there is a most. A prayer dangles over this bitter.

Looping coves of sympathy. How to history.

My flat speech in variously adopted professional tones.

Merger of you and me and take whatever you want.

Her beautiful poetry face. His intellectual arms.

I worry about the ferocious place in you while framing it.

A person as diversion, a thing beautiful, a small green-blue egg in a spring nest and now the field is gendered.

Have you seen the moment of last light? It means something to me.

Assuming my gender qualifies your hearing and therefore my speech, you overlap words with mine in what appears to be a neutral manner but your speech acts as solvent.

Down the hall, high heels as a metronome, watched.

Out of our bodies comes speech as clouds, flag, windsock, bandage.

Dear—
You could make more money if you wanted to. Such as a day of beauty, persuasive levels of caring. For example: doing both brow and lip.

Are you spending or quiet?

Let's go to lunch would mean exchanging speech and then carrying warm food in plastic bags.

Coherence as my mother sleeps after a complicated surgery.

And if I were, would you be generous with me as well?

Race ran the organization which one.

We socialize in this real estate of gerrymandered potlucks.

I think there exists silence as a legitimate response and I will say that now.

The caring for our souls by old black women in the narrative of a college president, passing. Excuse me for not knowing passing.

You remember but only after the spine is broken.

Something in chemistry called a suspension equals your ghosts caught in my air.

The Bronx is horning was a line they wrote where I was educated, teaching.

Responses to migration: the pullback of the form remains as a hum, a tongue.

VI.

Torchwood, a lexicon

TORCHWOOD

cascades the length of vesper-
light: totems

CLOISTER

yellowjackets in crooks—

CHIMERA

pagodas
cultivated by moonglow

CASEMENT

agape—
cartwheeling thought

GUIDEWORD

hoist, come about

ROSTRUM

sulking morning-glory—
wrenched from dusk

RATHE

trace of dormant, fruiting red

GLASSINE

tumbling epoch, strongest
paper

NETTLE

decidedly attached and many
nectars

IMPOST

from the widow's walk
tides pause

BREADFRUIT

toppling & pregnant

DOILY

edging—
blotter, fingered

DOG-EAR

furrows & petals—
far afield

CIRRUS

underpainting at the upward
edge

FILIGRE

taken from heaven
a flybook of webs and blunders

PALIMPSEST

of staggering trees
a pastiche, hewn

RELIQUARY

where polished or soft,
milkweed

FAN PALM

breadthwise ablaze—

VII.

Thinking a Kite

Thinking a kite

Thinking swifts

Thinking the bottom settles

Thinking between eggs

Thinking a wrapping

sadly thinking so reviews

Thinking answers

Thinking a scratch

Thinking to register the sound means

how to under thinking

buckled or pockets

Thinking sour while not so

I feel to say, walking

I feel against it, pressing

I feel toward today

I feel story

I feel sense

I feel fading

I feel you know what I mean

you will try

between

sitting at the edge while this

happens

happened

It is tender to family

It is tender to choose fading

It is tender to listen

Tender a noticing

Tender toward restless

to name

It is tender a hot shower in new places

It is tender a map of what is not said

wanting chords

Tender a rough history

of he and she

and she and you and so on

as anyone family

I feel a gift is difficult

Jill Magi, writer and visual artist, is the author of *Threads* (Futurepoem) and the chapbook *Cadastral Map* (Portable Press at Yo-Yo Labs). Her visual work, essays, poems, and prose have appeared in *HOW2*, *The Tiny*, *The New Review of Literature*, *Aufgabe*, *Jacket*, anthologized in *Fiction from the Brooklyn Rail* (Hanging Loose Press), as well as in the forthcoming books *Letters to Poets: Conversations on Poetry, Politics, and Community* (Saturnalia Press), *The Eco-Language Reader* (Portable Press at Yo-Yo Labs), and the *2008 Anthology of Younger Poets* (Outside Voices). Jill's visual work has been exhibited at the International Meeting of Visual Poetry, the Brooklyn Arts Council Gallery, and the Lower Manhattan Cultural Council 2007 Open Studios, where Jill was one of two writers-in-residence. She lives in Brooklyn, teaches at The Eugene Lang College and Goddard College, and runs Sona Books, a community-based chapbook press.

www.ingramcontent.com/pod-product-compliance
Lightning Source LLC
Chambersburg PA
CBHW030048100426
42734CB00036B/580